Porter
June '38

GREAT BRITAIN'S PART

GREAT BRITAIN'S PART

OBSERVATIONS OF AN AMERICAN VISITOR TO THE BRITISH ARMY IN FRANCE AT THE BEGINNING OF THE THIRD YEAR OF THE WAR

BY
PAUL D. CRAVATH

D. APPLETON AND COMPANY
NEW YORK   LONDON
1917

Copyright, 1917, by
D. APPLETON AND COMPANY

Printed in the United States of America

PREFACE

THE following observations were prepared for the *New York Times,* in which they first appeared. I have acquiesced in the suggestion that they be published, in the hope that they may aid a few Americans to a better appreciation of the greatness of England's achievements in the European War. I instinctively hesitate to write about France, because her appeal to the sympathy and admiration of the civilized world is so direct and dramatic that no words of mine seem adequate for the telling of her story. I cannot help feeling that with England the case is different. The British people and press have so liberally exercised the Englishman's inalienable right to abuse the government that we in America often hear more of England's mistakes than of her achievements. As a result, there is, I find, real misapprehension among Americans as to England's part in the war. It is the hope of doing something towards removing this misapprehension that furnishes the excuse for the publication of these pages.

P. D. C.

February, 1917.

I

GREAT BRITAIN'S PART

I

AN invitation to visit the British war zone in France came quite unexpectedly after I had spent the greater part of July studying war conditions in England. I had seen a good deal of the British army at home. I had visited recruiting stations, training camps, munition factories, hospitals, and camps for German prisoners. I had heard the conduct of the war discussed from every conceivable angle—in the House of Commons, at public meetings, at the Clubs, around the dinner table, and at the street corner. Indeed, in London, one hears very little else. I had heard as much of criticism as of praise, doubtless because the critic usually has a taste for conversation and leisure to gratify it.

The more I saw of the army that was training in England, the keener became my ambition to see the army that was fighting in France. I had little hope of gratifying this ambition, because I had been told that, since the inauguration of the great "Push," visits to the front by civilians were rarely permitted. Finally some good friends in the war office concluded that as I had heard so much in England from the critics, it would be worth while to send me to the front to form my own opinions.

What I saw so completely revolutionized my conceptions of the war, based on what I had been able to hear and read, that I have concluded that by publishing my impressions I may help other Americans to a better appreciation of the transcendent importance of the war and of the unparalleled scale on which it is being waged.

At the time of my visit I had no idea of publishing my observations. I accordingly made no notes and my knowledge of military affairs is very limited. I can therefore do little more than give my impressions.

II

II

IT would be hard to overstate the unpreparedness of England on that fateful fourth day of August, 1914, when she declared war against Germany. It will be to her everlasting glory that she responded so promptly to the call of duty without stopping to count the cost. She was not only wanting in all of the material preparations for war on land, but neither her government nor her people had any real conception of the colossal demands that the war would make upon the manhood and resources of the Empire. Anyone who has traveled in Germany or France can appreciate in some degree the magnitude of the task which confronted England, when he realizes that before she could really be a factor in the war on land it was necessary to build up a military organization in all of its manifold departments, practically equaling, in proportion to her population, the establishments which it had taken Germany and France half a century to create. She not only had to provide the material equipment for several millions of soldiers, such as barracks, training camps, ammunition factories, artillery, apparel, supplies of every kind and even the rifles which her soldiers were to carry, but she had the even more difficult task of arousing the war spirit in a people who from time immemorial had been trained in the occupations of peace.

How little the leaders of England

realized what was before them is shown by the division of opinion in the Government during the first days of the war as to whether *any* army should be sent to France. Kitchener's first call was for only a hundred thousand men. The second call was for half a million. Even after the war had fairly started and the Germans were swarming before the very gates of Paris, less than half a million men were in training. The failure to make even a fair beginning in providing for the necessary munitions, until the lack of them was revealed by the terrific slaughter in the second battle of Ypres in the ninth month of the war, was due to the Government's inability to grasp the scale on which the war was being waged by Germany.

When one realizes all this, England's

achievements at the close of the second year of the war seem little short of miraculous. They certainly are without parallel in history. In two years, or, if one allows for the wasted first months, in less than a year and a half, while maintaining, and even enlarging in the face of serious losses, the greatest navy the world has ever known, England, with the aid of her colonies, created, trained, equipped and munitioned an army of considerably over four million men. Of this army approximately half a million were furnished by Canada, Australia, New Zealand and South Africa. Most remarkable of all, it was chiefly a volunteer army, for conscription did not come until the war had lasted for over a year and a half, when from eighty to ninety per cent of the men of England, Scotland, Wales and Ulster and many from the rest of Ireland had volunteered.

Although at the time of my visit the British were maintaining an army of about a million and a half men in France and at least half a million more in the East and must have lost three or four hundred thousand men in killed, wounded and prisoners, England was still a veritable armed camp. Soldiers were everywhere. Each district had its training camp. There were about two hundred thousand men in training on Salisbury Plain alone and as many more at Aldershot and at the training camps where the Canadian regiments were concentrated. There were probably between a million and a half and two million soldiers in various stages of training throughout the United Kingdom.

Half the men one saw in the music halls and theaters and on Piccadilly and the Strand were soldiers, and on all the main thoroughfares within many miles of London military traffic predominated. The military hospitals in the United Kingdom were numbered by the hundreds. New munitions factories covering many square miles of land had been erected and most of the factories capable of producing munitions had been taken over by the Government until over four thousand factories were devoted in whole or in part to the manufacture of munitions of war. In addition to upward of four million men employed directly in the army and navy, between two and three millions more were engaged in activities exclusively or chiefly connected with the war. These gigantic activities were conducted by two great governmental departments with headquarters in London, the War Office and the Ministry of Munitions.

I shall not deal with the Ministry of Munitions, because its function is the *production* of munitions, the *use* of which in the conduct of the war is under the control of the army.

III

III

IT was on the seventeenth day of August that, armed with my "white pass" issued by G. H. Q. (General Headquarters) in France, I boarded a military train at Charing Cross Station. The routes for France via Folkstone and Boulogne and Dover and Calais had been taken over by the War Office, so that practically their entire traffic was military. My train carried General Sir Sam Hughes, War Minister of Canada, and his Staff, who were on their way to visit the Canadian troops, which constitute part of the British Army in France. The fleet which left Folkstone three hours later consisted of two transports carrying about three thousand troops, two hospital ships and a third transport, on which I was a passenger, which carried officers, Red Cross nurses, surgeons and civilian employees. The fleet was convoyed by two torpedo boat destroyers to protect it from German submarines.

When we were halfway across the Channel we passed a similar fleet coming in the reverse direction.

Although there seems never to have been a mishap to a military transport between England and France, we were all required to wear life preservers, and a queer looking lot we were. A dapper officer wearing a dirty life preserver across his chest and smoking a cigarette as he walks up and down the deck is one of the most humorous creations of the war.

Our voyage across the Channel was uneventful. We saw no signs of German submarines. The rumor is that the path of the transports plying between Folkstone and Boulogne is so well protected that it is almost impossible for submarines to approach. When we reached Boulogne I was met by an English Major, with whose aid I soon completed the necessary formalities with the French Aliens' and Customs' officials. On the pier I was turned over to an alert young Lieutenant in khaki, who announced that it was his job to look after me for the next three days.

Boulogne seemed more like a British military camp than a French city. On the piers and in the streets nearby were thousands of British soldiers, hundreds of lorries (motor trucks), ambulances and other military conveyances all painted a dull gray, and enormous quantities of munitions, provisions and war supplies of every kind. Boulogne is one of the chief distributing centers for the British army in France. It has a number of hospitals, enormous depots for supplies and that essential of every British military settlement, an Officers' Club. My guide said there was no time to see the sights of Boulogne, for, if we did not start at once, we would be late for tea—a calamity which any well-ordered Englishman will avoid at all hazards.

We were soon out of Boulogne in a gray army motor car. After motoring for about an hour on perfect roads through a smiling and peaceful countryside we reached a picturesque little city which before the war had no importance, except as the center of a prosperous agricultural community. "This," said my guide, "is G. H. Q." In England I had heard G. H. Q. spoken of scores of times, but I had never been told the name of the mysterious city in which it was located. It is one of the rules of the War Office that the location of G. H. Q. is never to be mentioned by the initiated. Theoretically, no civilian ever knows where anybody is in the British army in France.

If your friend is at General Headquarters, he never mentions the name of the city. Your letters to him are simply addressed to G. H. Q. If your friend is in the ranks, he will give you the name of his army corps and his regiment, but never the name of the place where he is stationed. Your letters to him are addressed to B. E. F. (British Expeditionary Force) and, with surprising promptness, they reach him wherever he happens to be.

Our motor stopped before a charming inn in the courtyard of which a score or more of British officers and a few French officers were having their tea under the shade of the Virginia creeper vines which hung in festoons above. We were greeted by a Captain who announced that tea was ready. After chatting for half an hour with a group of officers around the tea table we resumed our journey toward the Front.

IV

IV

IT will simplify my narrative if I explain briefly the organization of the British army. The supreme authority in the conduct of Great Britain's share in the war throughout the world, is the War Council,* which in August consisted of the Prime Minister, the Secretary of State for War, the

* The War Council of the new Cabinet as announced on December 9 includes the Prime Minister, David Lloyd George, Earl Curzon, Lord President of the Council and Government Leader in the House of Lords, Andrew Bonar Law, Chancellor of the Exchequer, Arthur Henderson, leader of the Labor Party, and Viscount Milner. The last two are without portfolios.

First Lord of the Admiralty and other members of the Cabinet. The War Council deals only with broad questions of policy.

The immediate direction of the war is under the General Staff in London, of which General Sir William Robertson is Chief and Major General Robert H. Whigham Deputy Chief. The General Staff has supervision of all the armies of England. Each of the forces in the various parts of the world has its own Commander in Chief who takes his orders from the General Staff in London. It is with the British Expeditionary Force in France that my observations deal. Its Commander in Chief is General Sir Douglas Haig, who in turn has a staff of several officers, each in charge of an important department of the army's activities.

G. H. Q., which we were visiting, is the administrative center of the army, as distinguished from what may be termed the fighting center, which is at Advanced G. H. Q., nearer the front, where General Haig and those of his staff who have to do with the actual conduct of the fighting are stationed. At G. H. Q. are the Quartermaster General in charge of supplies, the Surgeon General in charge of hospitals, the Chief of Transportation, and the heads of the various other departments which may be termed the business departments of the army. Compared with the British army, regarded as a business enterprise, the Standard Oil Company with its seventy-five thousand employees, the Pennsylvania Railroad Company with two hundred and forty thousand and the United States Steel Corporation with two hundred and fifty thousand, are mere pigmies.

The magnitude of the administrative responsibilities centered at G. H. Q. will be apparent when it is remembered that the British army in France consists of about a million and a half of men and each day suffers wastage varying from several hundred to several thousand men, most of whom are taken back to England for convalescence, while other men from England fill their places. In order to maintain the force at the front, it is necessary to bring an average of three or four thousand men from England each day and almost as many must be taken back. As the force in France is enlarged the number of men transported from England is correspondingly increased. The transport service comprises a large fleet of channel steamers, numerous railroad trains, barges on rivers, twenty-five or thirty thousand lorries and thousands of ambulances and motor cars. There are also three or four hundred thousand horses and mules and tens of thousands of horse-drawn vehicles, including ammunition wagons and artillery. Most of the provisions and supplies for the feeding, clothing and maintenance of this enormous army, and all of its munitions, must be transported from England. There are hundreds of hospitals in France filled with British wounded and scores of training camps. There are many sub-centers of activity such as Amiens, Rouen, Havre, Abbeville,

St. Omer, Boulogne and Calais. All of these activities are directed from G. H. Q. in the quiet little village in which we were taking tea with nothing about us to suggest war except the uniforms of the officers.

V

V

WE did not have time to visit the buildings in which G. H. Q. conducted its operations. We were told we would find them very much like the offices of any other great business, with hundreds of clerks, divided into departments, each with its administrative head. After leaving G. H. Q. we motored for about two hours by well tilled farms and through quiet villages where the only signs of war were the paucity of young men, the many women in mourning and the haunted look on the faces of the women and children. We reached Amiens just in time for dinner. Here, within a few miles of the present front, center many of the activities of the British Expeditionary Force and of General Foch's army, the most westerly of the French armies. Here is the headquarters of the British Intelligence Department and of the war correspondents, of whom at the time of my visit there were five for the British press and one for the American press. It is usually from Amiens that civilian visitors are taken to the Somme front of both armies.

The dining room of the Hotel du Rhin was a scene of great animation. It was crowded as it had never been crowded before the war. Most of the hundred or more diners were officers, chiefly British. There were several French officers and a few visitors from the Russian army. I could not help contrasting Amiens at the height of the British Advance in 1916 with Brussels in 1815 before the Battle of Waterloo as described by Byron and Thackeray. There was no "sound of revelry," there were no Amelias and Rawdon Crawleys, for women, unless they are Red Cross nurses, are not allowed to visit the British front, and there were no civilian hangers-on. The streets of the city were dark and deserted and there were no lights in the windows. A more complete absence of gayety and revelry could not be imagined. At Amiens we began to realize that modern war is grim, businesslike and unromantic.

Early next morning our party started in our gray Government motor car for the actual front. My traveling companion was Joseph Reinach, of Paris, the most important of the French historians of the war, whose daily commentaries contributed to the *Figaro* under the name of "Polyle" already amount to half a dozen volumes. Our faithful guide sat next to our soldier-chauffeur. Although Amiens was in the possession of the Germans for a short time during the first month of the war, it had suffered very little. It was full of soldiers, both French and English, and of lorries, ambulances, artillery and war equipment of every kind.

We motored several miles through a rural district which showed little evidence of the ravages of war. The Germans had occupied it for such a brief period during their first advance and during their retreat from the Marne that they left but few scars and most of those had disappeared. Soon the swarms of British soldiers in the villages made us realize that we were nearing the Front. In France the soldiers who are not actually in the trenches do not, as a rule, live in tents but are "billeted" in the villages. To make room for them the civil population is reduced and sometimes almost entirely excluded so that in the average village within a few miles of the British Front one sees more English soldiers than French peasants.

The British Tommies are very popular in the French villages, particularly with the ladies. They are gallant, good-natured and liberal with their money. Though they are the worst linguists in the world, they have been able to develop surprisingly effective means of communication. They are gradually creating an Anglo-French dialect which serves in France very much the same purpose that pidgin English does in the Orient. The streets of the villages occupied by the British have been renamed for the occasion. One is startled to see in a village which looks as unlike England as a French village can look, such signs as Rotten Row, Leicester Square, Piccadilly and Park Lane. At first I did not understand why soldiers were so abundant many miles back from the firing line. Our guide explained that only a small part of the British army in France is actually in the trenches at any particular time. The larger part of the army was in the villages and encampments at the rear. Some of these soldiers were resting after their week in the trenches; others were waiting their turn to enter the trenches and still others, recently arrived from England, were receiving the finishing touches of their training.

Soon the signs of the near proximity of the front became more numerous. The sound of distant cannonading grew louder and louder. Captive balloons began to appear on the horizon. The whirring of the flying machines was in the air. Soldiers were not only in the villages but in encampments on either side of the road, and in the fields were thousands of horses and mules, some belonging to the artillery, some to the cavalry, and others to the transport service.

We occasionally passed fields covered with artillery undergoing repairs or waiting to be moved to the front. Other fields were covered by enormous quantities of ammunition and supplies of all kinds, sometimes under sheds, but more frequently covered with canvas or wholly unprotected. Long lines of lorries, ammunition wagons, artillery and ambulances passed us, some moving toward the front and others moving toward the rear. As we approached nearer the front this traffic became an almost continuous procession, so that our own progress was very slow.

Here and there motors carrying officers and messengers on motorcycles dashed in and out. Every now and then we passed a group of German prisoners repairing the road. They did their work with sullen industry under the eyes of cheerful Tommies, who made no concealment of their liking for their jobs. In the ambulances we could see dimly outlined behind the curtains the forms of the wounded, those severely wounded lying on stretchers, the others sitting on benches. We began to meet decimated battalions of grim, battle-stained soldiers returning to their billets at the rear after days of hard fighting in the trenches and to pass fresh battalions of jaunty, swaggering Tommies moving in the opposite direction to take their turn on the firing line. They marched with the dash and enthusiasm which are so characteristic of the British soldier, singing songs and cracking jokes as though they were on their way to a picnic, instead of one of the most sanguinary battlefields the world has ever known.

Just before we reached Albert we stopped on an eminence from which we could see the panorama of fields and villages extending for several miles. A scene of more intense human activity could hardly be imagined. The vehicles in the long processions that were winding their way on every road were numbered by the thousands and as far as one could see in every direction there was a seething mass of men and vehicles and horses, broken here and there by great piles of the materials of war. It was like a gigantic ant heap. At first we received the impression of great disorder and confusion, but on closer observation we saw that every man had his place and every movement its purpose.

Finally we reached Albert. At the

time of the commencement of the "Push" this village was just behind the British front trenches. It had been the center of intense fighting and had been almost completely demolished by the shelling to which it had been so often subjected. Most of its buildings were destroyed. None had escaped injury. Like other villages, Albert swarmed with soldiers and war traffic. It had lost its entire civil population and was too badly battered even to provide billets. It is now famous for its church. In accordance with their predilection for sacred buildings, the Germans had centered their shell fire against Albert upon the church. All the buildings were destroyed. The main part of the edifice was completely shattered, but the spire surmounted by the statue of the

Virgin was still standing. This statue had toppled over, but remained aloft, held firmly to its pedestal. There is a pious belief that the Virgin of Albert is protected by divine intervention as an inspiration to the French Army, and that when she finally falls to the ground the war will have ended.

VI

VI

FROM Albert we worked our way through the dense traffic to the ruins of Fricourt, which before the "Push" was within the German lines. This village is so completely in ruins that hardly one stone is left standing on another. The oldest inhabitant would find it difficult to identify the spot where his house had stood. Even the roads and streets had disappeared under the débris and new roads had been cut through by the British army to provide a passage for their troops and supply trains.

Just after we left Fricourt we were startled by a tremendous explosion at the roadside and a concussion of air which almost upset us. We looked around in the direction from which the sound had come and detected a whiff of smoke coming out of an innocent looking clump of bushes a few yards away. This told the story. A British ten-inch gun had fired a shell over us toward the German lines. After motoring a few minutes more we left our motor behind a bank which protected it from German shells and continued our journey on foot.

We walked about a mile toward the German lines over a terrain which had recently been a network of German trenches. We reached an elevation from which we could survey the entire area of thirty or forty square miles which had been the center of the Battle of the Somme since the first of July.

Before the war this had been an ordinary rural district with rolling hills and undulating farms, interspersed with small forests and occasional villages. It now presented a scene of devastation and desolation that beggars description.

Before the advance of the British infantry, every portion of this territory had been subjected to a terrific shelling which had completely destroyed the network of German trenches except the underground chambers. The entrances to them had been covered with débris. There was hardly a square yard that had not been broken up by the explosion of mines or shells. The land bore every sort of wound, from craters a yard or so in diameter made by the explosion of the ordinary eighteen pounder shell, to the big mine craters, one of which was four or five hundred feet long and over a hundred feet wide. The German trenches had become great rough furrows of shattered earth. Bits of broken shells and unexploded shells and grenades were scattered broadcast. The trees in the woods had not only been denuded of their branches and leaves but their very trunks had been shattered and splintered. The villages and farm buildings had been so completely demolished that nothing was left to mark their locations but piles of broken and pulverized stone, brick and mortar.

Never in this or in any other war has any tract of land been subjected to shelling of anything like the intensity of that which had centered upon the area before us. It will be difficult, even for the industrious and thrifty French peasants, to restore this area to cultivation.

From our viewpoint we were able to see the activities of the British army for several miles of the Somme front. To the south of us, as far as we could see, were the enormous aggregations of men, vehicles and military supplies which I have already described. On the roads in all directions we could see the long processions winding their way to and from the front like enormous serpents. Just back of us were batteries of heavy British guns which could be heard but not seen, for they were hidden behind natural or artificial screens. There was a steady cannonading from many of these batteries, over our heads, to the German lines. The sound of the British guns behind us was disconcerting enough, but it was nothing compared with the weird, indescribable, crescendo shriek of the German shells which were dropping about us and exploding as they fell.

On the ridge a mile or so to the north we saw the British and German trenches running parallel with one another, often almost meeting. We could see the ruins of the villages which the British had recently captured and still further on, the villages which the Germans still held. We could not see the German guns. They were concealed behind the ridge, but the shrieking and exploding shells told us that they were there.

A mile or two to the south, against the horizon and a thousand feet or more above the ground, were the captive observation balloons of the British, familiarly known as "saucisses." We counted fifteen of them. To the north we could see an occasional German saucisse. Every now and then we heard the hum of the British aëroplanes above us. We could not actually see the men in the trenches, but we heard the small artillery and the patter of the machine guns. We were surrounded by the remains of German trenches, in the capture of which a few weeks before, tens of thousands of lives had been lost. It may well be that the German General was right who recently said that every square mile of territory captured by the British on the Somme had cost at least five thousand men. It is impossible to describe the emotions which this scene inspired. Every previous experience in one's life, every earlier conception of human achievement, seemed pale and colorless in comparison.

It will naturally occur to the reader to ask how a visitor could safely venture into the very center of such a conflict. Strange as it may seem, we had no sense of fear, and, what is stranger still, our guide assured us that we were in no danger. We were too far from the trenches to be within reach of the fire of the German rifles, machine guns and small artillery. It was only the shells from the German heavy artillery that were falling about us. Our guide said that we were safe on our hill because the Germans never shelled it in the morning. They were then shelling the farm, where we were to go that afternoon to watch the shells drop on the hill where we were then standing. Sure enough in the afternoon we stood by the fresh shell craters at the farm in the valley and watched the shells dropping on the hill which had been our point of observation in the morning. This habit of the Germans of shelling particular places at particular times, day after day, has been noted by many visitors to the front. It can be explained only by the German devotion to system and routine.

We spent an hour with one of the British batteries of heavy guns, which had been firing over our heads. Stopping on the roadside, where there was nothing to suggest the proximity of artillery, we walked a few rods through the bushes and found ourselves in a clearing two or three hundred feet in diameter, in which were two enormous ten-inch naval guns. At the side of each was a pile of shells, partly high explosives and partly shrapnel. There were tents and huts for the men, and in one corner there was a small portable house which was the office of the Major in charge of the battery. Here were his records and his maps showing the enemy's lines. He said that he had just been ordered to fire twenty rounds and that we were welcome to look on.

A dozen men manning each gun under the charge of a non-commissioned officer proceeded to set their guns and load and aim them. They then withdrew to a distance of about twenty feet and on the command of the officer in charge the gunner pulled his cord and *boom* went the gun, with a recoil of several feet.

The men then rushed forward and with crowbars restored the gun to its position and the operation of loading, aiming and firing was repeated at intervals of three and four minutes.

I asked the Major if he knew at what object he was firing. He said that he hadn't the slightest idea. All he knew was that he had received an order to shell a point on the enemy's lines about four miles distant, the elevation and location of which had been furnished him by the higher officer from whom he received his instructions.

The work of the gunner in charge of modern heavy artillery is exceedingly unromantic. He frequently neither knows what he is firing at nor whether his shells are hitting the mark. The object to be shelled is selected by an officer who may be several miles away. He, in turn, usually receives the data which guide him either from the observers in the saucisses or from the flying men who have been over the enemy's lines. All the men who have to do with the artillery fire in a given district have topographical maps divided into squares which are lettered or numbered. An observer in an aëroplane or in a saucisse reports to his proper superior officer that at a particular point on a designated square there is an enemy artillery emplacement or some other object to be shelled.

He reports his observations as to the direction and force of the wind at the particular time and place. With the aid of his topographical map the artillery officer can determine the elevation and location of the point in question. After making the proper allowance for the deflection of the shell caused by the wind, he is in a position to direct the officer in charge of the battery at what angle and at what elevation he shall aim his gun.

A message may come from the airmen or from the observers in the saucisses that the shells are falling wide of the mark, whereupon the officer who is directing the fire telephones the officer in charge of the gun to correct his aim accordingly. The precision with which the gunner who cannot see his mark is able to drop the shells at the desired spot is almost uncanny. The French artillerymen have for years been noted for their skill and efficiency. The promptness with which the British have developed artillerymen who rival those of the French and German armies is one of the surprises of the war. Military critics agree that the work of the British artillery during the latter part of the advance on the Somme has been most thorough and efficient.

VII

VII

ONE of our most interesting hours was spent at the headquarters of the Flying Corps of the Fifteenth Army Corps. Here were a large number of aëroplanes, both monoplanes and biplanes, of various types and sizes, comfortably housed in large tents. The duties of the airmen are varied. Some of them take photographs of the enemy's trenches, using aëroplanes specially designed for the purpose. It is the duty of others to locate the enemy's artillery emplacements and furnish data to guide their own artillerymen in shelling the enemy's lines. Some drop bombs, while others, with very rapid machines, fly further and watch the movements of the enemy. Some have machines which carry small guns and are especially fitted for fighting. It is their duty to protect the aëroplanes of their own army from the enemy and to engage and endeavor to destroy or drive off hostile aëroplanes which appear over or near their own lines. Most of the aëroplanes carry wireless telegraph instruments by which they communicate with their bases.

The British and the French now greatly excel the Germans in the efficiency of their air service. The native dash, courage and resourcefulness of the English and French make them admirable aviators. The English and French armies have more applicants for their aviation service than they can accept, while the Germans are compelled to offer special inducements to keep their aviation corps filled. On the western front the Germans have almost literally been driven from the air. They rarely appear over the lines of the Allies, and if a British or a French aviator wants a fight he usually has to go over the German lines to get it. During August one hundred and twenty German flying machines were destroyed on the western front as against about sixty on the side of the Allies.

While we were visiting the aviation headquarters an orderly handed to the pilot who was showing us around a telephone message which proved to be an order from headquarters to take photographs of some new German trenches. He remarked rather carelessly, "Those amateurs at G. H. Q. seem to think I can take photographs in a fog." He told the orderly to tell Bill (his mechanician) to "bring her out" and he walked off as carelessly as though he were going to take a drive in the park. An hour later when we were back at Fricourt, within two or three miles of the German trenches, our guide called our attention to a speck in the sky above us and remarked, "There goes our friend the aviator to get his photographs of the German trenches." By this time the fog had lifted and he undoubtedly got what he was after.

The development of the flying service has been one of the great achievements of the Allies in the war. Their superiority in this regard has given them an advantage which is increasing as the war progresses. I was surprised to learn that the proportion of men lost in the flying service is much less than among the junior officers in the active regiments at the front. The flying man has one great advantage. He either comes through alive and with glory or is killed outright.

The saucisses or captive balloons form a very important part of the air equipment of a modern army. Whenever it is clear enough for observations they are kept in the air at varying elevations. The observer suspended in the basket below a saucisse has a most monotonous task but a highly important one. He must be on the alert to observe and telephone to headquarters all significant movements of the enemy, and also to furnish data to guide the gunners of his own army in landing their shells at vulnerable places within the enemy's lines. The observer in a saucisse on the side of the Allies is comparatively safe because he is rarely molested by German airmen. The German saucisses, on the other hand, are frequently shot down by the airmen of the Allies. If a saucisse is destroyed there is a break in the monotony of the observer's existence when he opens his parachute and jumps off. He may drop comfortably to earth if the air happens to be still. He may be blown in any direction, even over the enemy's lines, if there happens to be a wind.

VIII

VIII

THERE is no department in the British army so thoroughly organized as its medical and hospital service. We spent an extremely interesting afternoon in visiting a series of hospitals, which gave us an idea of how the British wounded are cared for from the time they fall until they reach the convalescent hospitals in England. At the very front is the Regimental Aid Post, to which the regimental doctor and his stretcher bearers take the wounded men from the trenches or from "No Man's Land" where they have fallen, to get their first dressing. On an active section of the front the Regimental Aid Post is in the trenches or in connecting dugouts. After receiving their preliminary dressing the wounded men are carried by the stretcher bearers back to the Advanced Dressing Station, which is usually a mile or two toward the rear, beyond the reach of rifle and machine gun fire, but within the shelling line.

An Advanced Dressing Station must therefore be as inconspicuous and sheltered as possible, so as not to invite shell fire. The station which we visited was in a mine crater sixty or seventy feet in diameter. The floor had been leveled and covered with canvas painted to look like the surrounding earth. Thus a circular chamber about sixty feet in diameter was provided in which there was room for about seventy stretchers.

This crater happened to adjoin a series of remarkable German dugouts, which, on being cleaned out, furnished excellent living quarters for the doctors and men who acted as nurses. After the wounded brought from the Regimental Aid Post by the stretcher bearers have been examined and given such temporary treatment as they require, they are sorted for distribution among the various hospitals. As promptly as possible they are placed in motor ambulances and taken to the proper hospital.

We next visited a Casualty Clearing Station four or five miles further back. This was a hospital of tents covering several acres of a large field. Each tent was about thirty feet wide and sixty feet long and corresponded to a ward in a hospital. There were four operating tents, each with a receiving tent adjoining it. The operating tents were equipped with electric light, apparatus for administering anesthetics, hot and cold water, and all the appliances which one expects to find in a modern hospital.

As soon as a wounded man has been operated upon he is moved into a rest tent, from which he is transferred as soon as practicable, usually within twenty-four hours, to a base hospital. The theory of the organization of the field hospital service of the British army is to get the wounded men to the Advanced Dressing Stations as promptly as possible, give them their operations before there has been time for septic poisoning or gangrene to set in and then transfer them to the base hospitals where they are to remain until they are convalescent.

In the Advanced Dressing Station which we visited, twelve surgeons had operated during the previous thirty hours on nine hundred men, most of whom had severe wounds. With few exceptions these men had already been sent to other hospitals. A few miles further back we found a large village filled with hospitals. One was a rest hospital for the "walking cases," those slightly wounded or ill who would probably soon go back to the trenches. Another was a casualty clearing station which dealt with a class of cases different from those treated at the station nearer the front which we had previously visited. In it patients were received whose wounds were such that they could not be removed to the rear immediately after their operations.

Every day large numbers of men who are slightly wounded or convalescent are moved by trains or river barges to the hospitals at Havre, Rouen, Amiens, Abbeville and other French cities in the British zone or are taken to Boulogne or Calais, where they are transferred to hospital ships which take them to England.

At the time of my visit to the British front the busiest people connected with the army seemed to be the surgeons. Since the first of July the casualties had averaged over three thousand a day and there were periods when they exceeded ten thousand a day. It is said that during one week in July the *daily* British casualties on the Somme exceeded the entire casualties of the Allies in the Battle of Waterloo. Yet, so perfect was the medical and hospital service of the British army that it never broke down under this terrific pressure.

The bravery of the wounded men in the hospitals is past belief. I must have seen more than a thousand wounded men, some on stretchers fresh from the battlefield, some waiting their turn on the operating table, some who had just left it, some hovering between life and death, and others in various stages of convalescence, but never did I hear a moan or a whimper. The war has developed a new kind of courage. Fortitude and ability to bear suffering patiently seem to be in the air.

Once in a British hospital I noticed a young Tommy in tears. I was told that he had just arrived from the front severely wounded. His face was pale and drawn.

I said to myself, "Here at last is a wounded man who has broken down under the strain." But when the nurse spoke to him on the assumption that his wounds were the cause of his tears he said, showing plainly that his feelings were hurt, "It isn't my wounds that trouble me. I was just thinking of my hard luck. The Huns got me the first day I was in the trenches before I had had a chance to get any of them."

IX

IX

WE saw German prisoners under all conceivable conditions —mending the roads, in workshops where they were plying their trades, at work in the fields, eating their dinner in their camps and listening to the music of their own bands. While it is hardly fair to form one's opinion of Germany at war from the demeanor of prisoners, a few inferences are irresistible. One is that there is a distinct breaking down of the morale of the German army on the western front. This is indicated by the increasing willingness of German soldiers to be captured and by the admissions of many prisoners, not only in conversation after capture, but in their letters to their friends, that they have begun to realize that the truth has been kept from them and that Germany is not winning the war. Many of them said that they were quite contented in the comfortable German trenches until the "Push" began, but that from that time on their life was one continuous Hell, deliverance from which in any form whatsoever was welcome.

We were told everywhere that German prisoners are easy to manage, that they work willingly and show their military training by their obedience to discipline. They manage their own camps, cook their own food and repair their own clothes and shoes. The ordinary routine of discipline is administered by non-commissioned officers chosen from their own number.

At one prisoners' camp Mr. Reinach questioned an exceptionally intelligent German Sergeant Major regarding his views as to the cause of the war. He said that he and his comrades often talked about the cause of the war and that they were agreed among themselves that Russia started the war in order to get Constantinople; that France joined Russia because she wanted Alsace and Lorraine; and that England entered the war because she wanted to destroy Germany's commercial supremacy. He and his comrades could not understand why it was that when thousands of lives were being destroyed every day, the Allies should make such a fuss over the execution of Edith Cavell and of Captain

Fryatt, and, for that matter, they were equally at a loss to understand why their own Government was constantly harping on the *Barralong* case. The prisoners appeared wholly unconscious of the moral questions involved in the war. They apparently assumed that all the belligerents were prompted by self-interest and that any method of destroying an enemy was legitimate. Could there be a more authoritative and disingenuous statement of the Teutonic point of view?

I shall always carry one indelible impression of the German prisoners, and that is of the prevalence of a more or less clearly defined type of face—cruel, cunning, brutal and arrogant. It is the face which Raemaekers has immortalized. Whenever I think of a German prison camp that type comes to my memory with amazing distinctness. I have talked with so many other observers who have had the same experience that I feel sure that I cannot be wrong. At a large German prisoners' camp in England fifteen hundred prisoners, mostly young men from crack regiments captured during the early months of the war, were lined up before us.

Our party, excepting the Englishman from the Foreign Office who had us in charge, was made up entirely of neutrals. We were two Americans, one Greek editor, one Dutch correspondent and two Scandinavian journalists. After studying the faces of scores of the prisoners we withdrew and compared notes.

Each of us had reached the same conclusion, that never before had we seen a group of men in which so large a proportion of the faces were of one type—a type that suggested brutality and degeneracy. These men were not the Germans whom I had known at home and liked, nor the Germans I had met in my visits to Germany. We could not escape the conclusion that they were Prussian Janissaries, the product of two generations of militarism with all that goes with it. As we looked at these men we shuddered at the memory of the atrocities that they had committed in the villages of Belgium and northern France, and we realized, as we had never realized before, the fate from which the victory of the Allies will save Christendom—the people of Germany no less than the others.

X

X

WE were fortunate in having an opportunity of seeing something of the higher commands which were conducting the vast activities around us. As I have already said, General Sir Douglas Haig, the Commander in Chief of the British armies in France, is stationed at Advanced G. H. Q. The forces under his command are in turn divided into four armies, each in command of a General who looks to Sir Douglas Haig for his instructions. Each army consists of two or more army corps, each commanded by a General who looks for his orders to the General commanding the army of which his corps forms a part. Each army corps is divided into two divisions of about twenty thousand men each, commanded by a General who takes his orders from the Corps Commander. Each division is divided into three brigades commanded by Brigadier Generals who take orders from the division commander. Each brigade is divided into four battalions in the infantry and corresponding subdivisions for cavalry and artillery. The regimental unit practically disappears in the organization of the British army in the field.

Each one of these units has its headquarters. The administrative G. H. Q., as we have already seen, was at least forty miles back from the front. Advanced G. H. Q. was fifteen or twenty miles from the front, and at intervals nearer the portion of the front which we were visiting were the headquarters of the Fourth Army, of the Fifteenth Army Corps, of the three divisions constituting that corps and of its brigades. The battalion headquarters were in or near the trenches.

The first day of our visit we lunched at Advanced G. H. Q. with General Haig and his Staff. Leaving the battlefield just before noon, we motored back through Fricourt and Albert, by the processions of wagons, lorries and ambulances, turned off into a side road away from the military traffic and finally reached the little village in which Advanced G. H. Q. was located. Turning into a stately drive, we approached the château which is General Haig's headquarters. One could not imagine a less warlike scene. We were at least fifteen miles from the field of battle— far enough away so that on the day of our visit not even the cannonading could be heard. Children were playing upon the lawn, cattle were grazing in the neighboring meadow, flowers were blooming in the garden. There was none of the bustle and excitement that one associates with war.

Sir Douglas Haig and the members of his Staff who were gathered around the luncheon table acted and talked very much as one would expect the president of a railroad company, surrounded by his vice-presidents and heads of departments, to talk and act. This at first shocked one's sense of the fitness of things. The average man's conception of a great general is apt to be of a man with fierce countenance, knotted brow and flaming eyes, with the sweat of anguish or the glow of triumph on his face. One feels that if the Commander is not brandishing his sword and rushing into the midst of the fray to encourage his soldiers to do deeds of valor he should at least be surrounded by the smoke and din of battle. But here was a quiet, unassuming, clear-eyed gentleman, well groomed and faultlessly dressed, with no sword at his side and nothing to suggest the soldier except his uniform. He was surrounded by a dozen equally calm and matter of fact gentlemen. When the shock was over we realized that all this was as it should be, that after all the conduct of a modern military campaign is very much like the management of a colossal business, and that the Commander in Chief of a great army, like the head of a great business enterprise, must keep his head clear and his mind calm and be far enough away from the scene of action to be able to confine his attention to the great underlying questions and to leave the execution of details to his organization.

After lunch General Haig showed us his maps, profiles and records. I was very much struck with the completeness of his information regarding the strength, the movements and the plans of the Enemy. The Intelligence Service of the British army has attained a surprising degree of perfection and is said to excel that of the Germans. The information, gained in an infinite variety of ways, from spies, from observers in captive balloons, from flying men and their photographs, from German prisoners and from captured documents, reaches Headquarters in the form of conclusions in condensed form which are so accurate that they can be accepted without reserve. What daring, ingenuity, patience and sacrifice may be represented by a single page or a single chart that finally comes before the eyes of the Commander in Chief!

Later in the day we learned that while we were at lunch with General Haig one of the most lively engagements of the Somme advance had been in progress and had resulted in the capture of Delville Wood. All the arrangements for this engagement had been worked out in advance by General Haig and the Commander of the

Army Corps which was to be engaged. These arrangements were being carried out by subordinates and the mind of the Commander in Chief was free to plan the next move.

XI

XI

AFTER leaving Advanced G. H. Q. we motored again toward the front, passing the headquarters of the Fourth Army and finally reached the little village which was the headquarters of the Fifteenth Army Corps, where we were to take tea with the Corps Commander and his staff. Our motor stopped before an unpretentious two-storied house on the main street of the village, which proved to be the Corps headquarters. Our guide, leaving us in the courtyard, went upstairs to announce our arrival. He soon reappeared, accompanied by a junior officer, who asked me to follow him.

We entered a very simple second-story room, where we found the General surrounded by his staff. The walls and tables were covered with maps, which some of the officers were studying intently. It was manifest from the preoccupied air of all in the room that something was happening. The General greeted us and said, "Tea is off, for we are fighting a battle. You may watch us, but conversation is not encouraged." I sat around for half an hour watching the General and his staff at work. They were directing the battle which had been in progress all day and which was soon to result in the capture of Delville Wood. Not a sound of battle could be heard, but telephone and telegraph reports from the fighting line came in at frequent intervals. There were frequent consultations over the maps and frequent orders to the Front.

The General and the members of his staff were cool and deliberate, but we could see that the attention of each man was concentrated on the work in hand. We had a chance to see the maps and profiles of the terrain on which the fighting was taking place. They showed every hill and valley, each artillery emplacement, the location of the numerous trenches upon which the attack was being made and the disposition of the troops on both sides. With the aid of these and the reports which were being constantly received by telephone and telegraph, the General and his staff could follow and direct every phase of the battle.

This experience at the Corps Headquarters during the progress of a battle, following our visit to the scene of the actual fighting, enabled me to realize, as I had never realized before, why the commander of a modern army conducts a battle from his quiet headquarters many miles in the rear, where he can neither hear nor see the conflict. If he attempted to conduct it from the battle-field, he would be just as helpless as the president of the Pennsylvania Railroad Company would be if he attempted to operate his railroad system from a signal tower in Broad Street Station at Philadelphia.

If we had continued our journey to the firing line and visited the Division Headquarters and the Brigade Headquarters, and finally the Battalion Headquarters, we would doubtless have found at each the same intensity of concentration as at the Corps Headquarters. At the Battalion Headquarters in the trenches we would have found the Colonel and his officers, surrounded by the smoke and din of battle, executing the movements which were being guided from the quiet office of the Corps Commander several miles to the rear.

On the day after our visit to the headquarters of the Fifteenth Army Corps we lunched with the General commanding this Corps and his staff in their charming little sixteenth-century château. The battle of the day before had been fought and won, and our luncheon was so calm and normal that it was hard to realize that we were at a military headquarters.

XII

XII

NO visitor to the British army in France can fail to be impressed with its efficiency, the thoroughness of its organization, the vastness of its operations, the wonderful spirit of indomitable determination which pervades the men of every rank from the Commander in Chief down to the humblest worker in the army service corps. The officers of the British army in France do not, as a rule, suggest the type of officer that was so common in England before the war. It is clear that those in high command have been chosen for their efficiency and fitness.

"Pull" and social prominence and personal popularity, which are supposed to have been such potent factors in securing advancement in the British army in the past, have ceased to count. The officers whom I met seemed more like hard-working, serious-minded, practical men of business than the genial, sport-loving English gentlemen by whom the British army used to be so largely officered. Outside of the Colonial troops, most of the officers above the rank of Major had been in the regular army before the war, either in active service or upon the retired list. Actual service and responsibility have hardened and developed their characters.

On the other hand, comparatively few of the officers below the rank of Major had been in active service before the war. Only a handful of the junior officers of the original expeditionary force of one hundred and fifty thousand men which was sent to France during the first month of the war has survived. Their places have been filled, to some extent, by men promoted from the ranks, but, in the main, by young men from all walks of life who received their first serious military training after the beginning of the war. They are the best young men of the nation, the pick of the four million volunteers. What they lack in experience and training they make up in natural ability, earnestness, enthusiasm and devotion to duty, qualities in which the volunteer officer the world over is bound to excel.

One cannot resist a feeling of affection and admiration for the British

"Tommy." He has a peculiar quality of his own which is found in the soldier of no other nation. The few thousand survivors from the ranks of the original army have leavened the whole force, so strong and persistent and pervading are the traditions of the British army. The slouching yokels from the Counties and the stoop-shouldered, anemic clerks from London and Manchester have become dashing, swaggering "Tommies" with all the airs and graces of veterans. Their good humor amid discomfort and privation, their bravery in battle, their toughness of fiber, and their capacity cheerfully to face death and endure suffering give one a wholly new conception of the capacities of human nature.

Perhaps the most characteristic tradition in the British army is that of neatness and pride in one's personal appearance. An essential part of every British soldier's kit is his razor, and there is no regulation more sternly enforced than the rule requiring the daily shave of all of Tommy's face except his upper lip. I have been told that in the darkest hour of the early period of the war an order from the War Office was promulgated with great solemnity and thoroughness cautioning officers that there must be no relaxation in the order requiring a shaven face for all and a hairy upper lip for officers.

This order, ridiculous as it may seem, is part of the tradition which makes the English Tommy what he is and what no other soldier in the world has been able to become. The man who shaves every day is very apt to take a bath whenever he can, to stand up straight and to be careful of his personal appearance, which usually means being careful of his health. The result is that a battalion of Tommies march into the trenches as though they were on parade, and when the shattered remnants march out every man is still trying to look his neatest and his best.

The crowning marvel of it all is that this wonderful army was created in less than two years. England has demonstrated to the world that, so far as the men in the ranks are concerned, an efficient army can be created with a few months' training after obtaining officers and adequate equipment. Hundreds of thousands of British soldiers have been ready for the front after three or four months' training and comparatively few of them have had more than six months' training. These men compare favorably with the men in the original regiments which constituted England's seasoned army at the outbreak of the war.

England's experience has demonstrated that if a nation expects to be prepared for war and to rely chiefly upon a volunteer army, two things are essential for reasonably prompt mobilization. One is adequate equipment and organization for the production of munitions and supplies, and the other is an adequate body of trained officers. The lack of a sufficient number of trained officers was a handicap which England found it more difficult to overcome than the lack of munitions. One of the most prominent statesmen of England said to me: "Tell your friends in America that what they need most, if they expect to be in a position of military preparedness, is a sufficient number of staff colleges to produce enough trained officers to drill a volunteer army."

XIII

XIII

THE question is often asked, Why do General Haig and General Foch keep hammering away for months on the Somme front, where they have given the enemy such ample opportunity to organize a stubborn resistance? Why do they not surprise the Germans by an unexpected attack in force at some weak point in their line? The answer to this question is perfectly simple. An effective surprise attack on a large scale on the western front is impossible. Neither side can pierce the heavily intrenched line of the enemy without an intense bombardment by heavy artillery, for which weeks, per-

had lost most of my doubts. I thought I understood the policy which is behind the grim, unyielding, relentless campaign which General Haig and General Foch are waging on the Somme.

In the first place, they have destroyed some hundreds of thousands of Germans. The Germans are proclaiming that the casualties of the Allies are out of proportion to their own. My information is to the contrary, especially if one considers the eighty thousand German prisoners which the Allies have captured on the Somme since the first of July. Considering the fact that the Allies have lost few prisoners, and the frequency of the unsuccessful German counter attacks, my guess is that the losses on the two sides are not far from equal. Awful as the thought is, one of the tasks of the Allies, perhaps their chief task, is to destroy Germans and keep on destroying Germans. That they must do, whatever the sacrifice. If the work of destroying Germans lasts long enough the numerical superiority of the Allies will finally give them the advantage.

In the second place, the victories of the Allies on the Somme have gone far to break the morale of the German army. They have convinced the German soldiers that they are not invincible and that, on the western front at least, the Allies now excel the Germans in numbers, in artillery, in equipment and in all the qualities which go to insure victory.

Another great gain is that the Germans have been compelled to shift enormous numbers of troops to reinforce their armies on the Somme. There is reason to believe that at least half a million men were thus transferred during the first month of the advance. This was undoubtedly one of the causes, perhaps the principal cause, of the lessening pressure on Verdun and of the thinning of the Teutonic line in the East which made the successful Russian advance possible. When the history of the war is finally written it may well be that General Haig and General Foch, operating on the Somme, will be credited with a good share of the credit for the victories of the French before Verdun and of the success of General Brussiloff's drive in the East. And finally it is inevitable that before long the wide dent which the Allies are making in the

German line in Picardy will compel the Germans to withdraw from their present position in France and straighten their entire western line, at least from Picardy to the sea.

The average American with whom I talk about the war usually ends with the question, "Are you sure that the Allies will win?" No American with English or French blood in his veins will permit himself to ask that question after he has seen the British and the French at war. He *knows* the Allies will win. Perhaps he cannot give the reasons for his faith. We often cannot give the reasons for our strongest and soundest faith. I feel that the Allies *must* win because their cause is a righteous cause—because they are fighting for the salvation of Christendom. I believe they *can* win. Never before has the spirit of France shown so pure and bright as in this her hour of greatest trial. Notwithstanding the disproportionately heavy losses which her position forced upon her during the first two years of the war, she will continue to do, in proportion to her numbers, all that can be done by a nation of brave and devoted men and women led by the most skillful generals the war has produced. Fighting at her side is inexhaustible, unconquerable Russia—not the old Russia of the Czar and the Bureaucracy, but the Russian People, animated by genuine affection for France and by a patriotism which is akin to religious devotion. I cannot help feeling that in this third year of the war the greatest strength of the Allies is in

Great Britain, in her supremacy on the seas, in her rapidly growing armies, in the boundless wealth and resources of her Empire, in her dogged perseverance, in her indomitable courage, and, most of all, in that toughness of moral fiber which has so often brought her victory out of apparent disaster.

We shall doubtless continue to hear much of blunders that England is making and of blunders that she is not making, but some day the world will wake up to a realization that England and her Allies have won the war. Even then the critics in and out of Parliament will doubtless insist that the war was lost by the blunders of an incompetent government. That has always been England's way.

(1)